8/91   JN

D0468306

Looking Good

PUBERTY

by Jacqueline A. Ball

Rourke Publications, Inc.
Vero Beach, FL 32964

The author wishes to thank the following people for their help in the preparation of this book:

Eileen Griffin for her work on the illustrations in this book. Ms. Griffin is an artist, illustrator and the owner of a graphic arts company.

Dixie Montgomery, owner and director of a modeling school and agency.

© 1989 Rourke Publications, Inc.

Library of Congress Cataloging-in-Publication Data

Ball, Jacqueline A., 1952-
   Puberty / Jacqueline A. Ball.

      p.   cm. — (Looking good)

   Bibliography: p.
   Includes index.
   Summary: Explains how a girl's body changes during puberty, discussing the menstrual cycle, breast development, hormonal activity, and emotional changes.
   1. Adolescent girls—Physiology—Juvenile literature. 2. Puberty—Juvenile literature. 3. Menstruation—Juvenile literature. [1. Adolescent girls. 2. Puberty. 3. Menstruation.] I. Title. II. Series: Rourke, Arlene C., 1944- . Looking good.
RJ144.B35   1988   88-15754
612′.661—dc 19   CIP
ISBN 0-86625-283-5   AC

CONTENTS

WHAT'S HAPPENING TO ME, ANYWAY?

If you're like most girls your age, you've probably been asking yourself that question a lot lately. It's perfectly understandable. So much *is* happening to you.

Your body is changing.
Your feelings are changing.
Your moods seem to change a mile a minute.

All these changes can make you feel anxious and confused. They can make you feel awkward and ugly. They can make your whole world seem suddenly crazy and insecure.

It's a tough time for many young people. All these changes are perfectly normal, however. They're part of a dramatic process you're going through, called *puberty*. Another word for it is *adolescence*.

Puberty comes from the Latin word meaning "adult." The root of the word adolescence means "becoming." So you're *becoming* an *adult*. More specifically, becoming a woman.

It isn't an easy process, and it certainly isn't fast. In fact, it's quite slow. Female puberty usually lasts eight or nine years, starting with changes so deep and gradual that you can't even notice them. It's a stage that every girl must go through. Don't worry if you seem to be taking more or less time than your friends; everyone gets through it at her own speed. That's very important to remember: everyone's experiences with puberty are just a little bit different from everyone else's. That's because human beings are all unique.

4

Some girls have mature bodies at 12, while others still look like little girls until they are 16. Some girls may look like children, but be very grown up emotionally and intellectually. With other girls, the reverse is true.

You may be tempted to compare your development with other girls at this point in your life, but it won't do much good. Inside you is your own, special biological "clock." It's a timetable for growth that your body follows instinctively. It dictates what is "normal" for you. You can't reset it. It is already programmed, and cannot be changed. It's part of what makes you *you*.

Your experiences with puberty will be as special and unique as everything about you. With a little help, this topsy-turvy time can be exciting and full of discovery.

> **TIP:** Most girls are not fully developed until age seventeen or later. Don't worry if you're a slow starter. Give it time.

WHAT'S GOING ON OUTSIDE?

It may seem that all the changes you're going through are confused and pointless. Actually just the opposite is true. Your body is getting ready for a role only women can play — motherhood.

You will not have the maturity to raise a child for many years. Even so, your body starts to prepare for this role before you are born. You probably won't see any outward signs of the preparations until age 11 or 12. Remember, everybody's different.

Your Physical Self

The first thing you may notice is hair growth in a new place: your pubic area. Your body may go on a growing spree, shooting up several inches while putting on pound after pound. Your arms and legs may feel incredibly long.

The whole shape of your body starts changing. Your waistline nips in more. Your hips grow rounder. You notice the tiny buds on your chest that are the first signs of breasts.

Puberty has now officially begun.

As it continues, your nipples and breasts change and grow. You gain some more height and weight. Your body shows curves instead of little-girl straightness. Hair grows under your arms. The downy fuzz on your legs is now longer, and may be coarser and darker too.

Then everything slows. Your height and weight stabilize. Your shape is now rounded and womanly. Because that is, in fact, what you have become: a young woman.

Of course, it doesn't happen that easily. Along the way, these outward signs of puberty may make you uncomfortable. Some girls feel awkward and clumsy as they try to get used to their new height and their added weight. Some girls may feel embarrassed by their new breasts, especially if they're bigger or smaller than those of their friends.

Many girls actually hate their bodies at some point during puberty. Almost all girls are very shy about their bodies at this time. Being undressed in front of anyone — a doctor, your mother, even your best friend — can be pure agony.

TIP: If *you* feel self-conscious, try to remember that you're not alone. Other girls are feeling just as bashful as you.

If you are *not* self-conscious, be grateful. Be sensitive to the feelings of others. Your friends may be suffering. Don't make unflattering remarks about someone's body. Cutting remarks can wound deeply and leave lasting scars.

Breasts

You learned earlier that all the changes in puberty are leading up to one thing: the ability to become a mother. For this purpose also, nature gives a woman breasts. They contain the milk glands that will enable her to nurse her babies.

Breasts are more than functional. They are a very beautiful part of a woman's body. However, at your age, many girls don't think so. Far from finding their breasts beautiful, they are ashamed or embarrassed by them. They feel too flat or too top-heavy. Girls worry that their breasts are too pointed. They worry that their nipples are the "wrong" color or shape.

All this anxiety is because girls develop at greatly differing rates. Some girls go through the stages very quickly. Others take quite a few years. A lot depends on your heredity.

You don't really have much control over how your breasts are going to grow, or how fast. Exercise can only develop the pectoral muscle behind the breast, not the breast itself. Creams and lotions are a waste of money.

Breasts do need attention and care. First of all you should:

Wear a bra. After you've gone through the first stages of breast development, you should always wear a bra for daily activity. Take the time to get one fitted in the underwear or lingerie section of a good department store. When you find one that feels good and gives you a flattering line, buy several. Don't be afraid or ashamed to ask advice from the saleslady.

If you participate in sports, you may need extra support. Styles with straps that criss-cross in the back are especially good, because the straps won't slip down your arms. For sports that require a lot of running or jumping, try a jog bra.

If...

One breast starts growing before the other, don't worry, sometimes one grows first. The slower one will catch up.

You notice any discharge coming from a nipple, tell your doctor. It's probably just the fluid that keeps the ducts open. Many women have some breast secretion. To be on the safe side, ask about it.

Your nipples are pink, it's o.k.

Your nipples are brown, it's o.k.

You notice hair around your nipples, it's not a cause for alarm. However, don't risk irritation or infection by pulling them out. Don't even think of shaving them off! You could cut yourself. Again, ask you doctor what to do.

> **TIP:** Standing up straight will make your breasts look their best, regardless of their size.

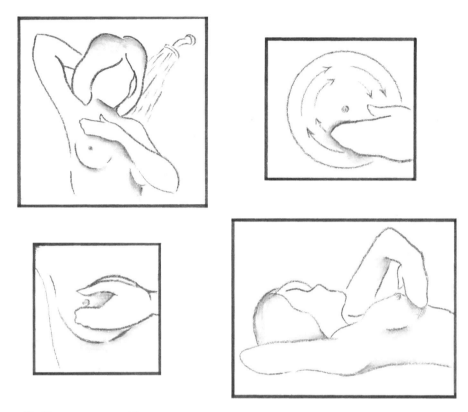

Self-examine. Breast cancer is not common in teenagers, but it is important to check for lumps or discharge and tell your doctor about any irregularities. At your age most lumps are caused by hormonal changes and activity or by build-up of fluid before your period. There's also a lump called an *adolescent nodule* that is common during puberty. It makes the nipple very tender, but it is not serious and usually goes away in time.

Here's how to self-examine. When you shower, feel every part of your breast. Touch yourself in a circular, clockwise motion searching for lumps. Squeeze each nipple, looking for discharge. The habit of self-examination is a good one to develop. It could save your life someday. Do breast examination about once a month.

WHAT'S GOING ON INSIDE?

The dramatic changes you're seeing outside are all caused by even more dramatic changes inside.

When you were born, like all baby girls, you arrived with millions of tiny eggs in your two *ovaries*. The ovaries are the female reproductive organs.

The eggs remain inactive for years. Then, at around age eight, something happens. The brain starts a process that produces a special hormone known as *FSH*. The hormone acts on the ovaries and the eggs begin to "wake up." Then the ovaries produce another hormone, *estrogen*. All this hormonal activity is what starts puberty. Nobody has yet figured out how the brain knows it's time to start the action. That is one of the miracles of human life.

Menstruation

A few years later, an important event occurs. It is called *menarche* (men-AR-kee.) It means that *menstruation* has begun. In other words, you get your first period. Menstruation usually begins between the ages of ten and sixteen. From now on, as far as your body is concerned, you will be able to become pregnant.

You've probably heard about menstruation by now, and perhaps you've started menstruating yourself. Lots of girls worry about their periods. There are so many myths and half-truths about the subject that it's easy to be scared.

PARTS OF THE FEMALE REPRODUCTIVE SYSTEM

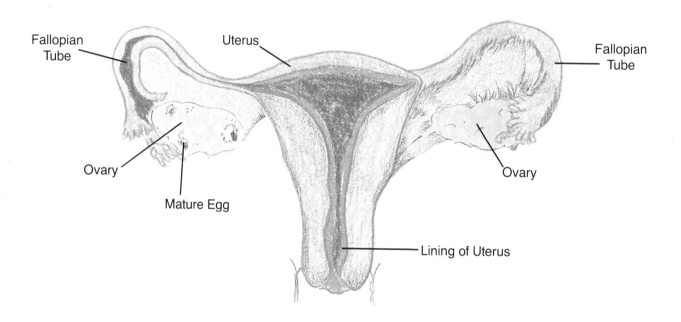

So first of all, relax! Don't be afraid. The whole menstrual process is perfectly normal. Having your period is a sign that you are healthy and that your body is working properly.

It is not disgusting, or bad, or unclean. If people tell you it is, don't listen. They are wrong, and they are silly.

Menstruation is simply the release of material that your body doesn't need any more.

Let's take a close look at the whole process leading up to this release. It's something that will happen *every* month from menarche until you're about 50 years old, except when you're expecting a baby. It is called your *menstrual cycle.*

A Menstrual Cycle

Each month, one of those millions of eggs you were born with ripens in one of your ovaries. This egg can become a baby.

The egg breaks out of the ovary. This is called *ovulation*. It happens about halfway through the month.

The egg starts a journey of a few days through the *fallopian tube* into the *uterus*. If it is fertilized by a sperm along the way, you can become pregnant.

Meanwhile, the lining of the uterus is preparing itself for a fertilized egg. The uterus is thick with soft tissue.

If your egg has been fertilized, it implants itself into the lining. There it will grow for nine months and become a baby.

If the egg has not been fertilized, it breaks apart and is released, together with the lining of the uterus. This makes the bloody discharge we know as *menstrual flow*.

> **TIP:** The whole process is perfectly natural, healthy and normal. Because we tend to think of blood as a sign of injury, it's hard to accept menstrual blood as a good sign, not a bad one. Remember, it *is* a good sign.

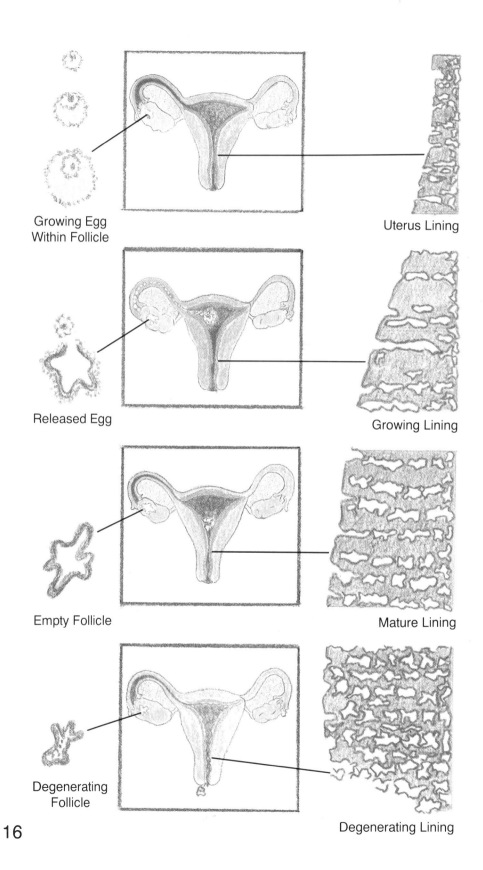

Growing Egg
Within Follicle

Uterus Lining

Released Egg

Growing Lining

Empty Follicle

Mature Lining

Degenerating
Follicle

Degenerating Lining

16

What's A "Normal" Period?

Menstrual cycles average around twenty-eight days. Ovulation generally occurs around the middle of the cycle. Some girls and women have longer or shorter cycles. "Normal" can have a wide range of meaning, from twenty-one to thirty-five days.

The flow can last anywhere from three to eight days, usually becoming heaviest on the second and third days. The flow may look very heavy at times, but you don't lose much blood — perhaps a half a cup during the entire period.

When you first start menstruating, you might skip two or three months before you have your next period. *Don't worry.* That's normal too. It's just your body trying to regulate the ovulation process. It will work itself out.

TIP: Stress can cause skipped cycles. Avoid unnecessary troubling situations. Exercise moderately to reduce stress. Talking things out helps, too.

Coping With Menstrual Problems

For most girls, having their period doesn't interfere with their daily lives. It's usually possible to participate in sports and be active every single day of the month.

Some girls do have cramps or other problems during or before their periods. They may feel depressed or grouchy. Their breasts may become sore and tender. They may retain water so that their ankles and fingers get puffy.

Consider making some changes in your routine, especially two weeks before your period.

Avoid salt and salty food. Diet drinks, prepared foods like hot dogs and frozen dinners and fast food all have large quantities of sodium (salt). Dried and canned soups are absolutely loaded with it. Salt makes your body retain water, so it makes bloating worse and can cause actual weight gain. Check labels on boxes for sodium content. You should have only 300-400 milligrams *per day.* Some soups have 900 milligrams *per cup!*

Eat plenty of fresh fruit and raw vegetables. Bananas and oranges are especially good. They have the potassium you need to fight off any feelings of weakness.

Get plenty of exercise. Exercise releases substances called *endorphins* that help you fight off depression and feel good.

Cramps Menstrual cramps can produce a dull ache in your abdomen, or a nauseated feeling. They're caused by the uterus tightening as it sheds its lining. They don't generally last more than a day or two, but tell your doctor if you're bothered by them. These measures may help:

Exercise. Any aerobic exercise such as walking, swimming, or aerobics class is particularly good.

Avoid coffee or anything containing caffeine. Caffeine makes *prostaglandins* in your body. These substances have been associated with cramps. Remember, most colas are high in caffeine.

Medication. Some over-the-counter medications can help. *Don't take any medicine without checking with an adult who is knowledgeable on the subject.* Even aspirin can have dangerous side effects. Generally speaking, try to deal with menstrual discomfort through changes in diet and exercise. Don't rely on medicine unless you really must.

Your Body's Special Needs

All teenagers, male and female, need plenty of **vitamins** and **minerals** and forty-five to fifty grams of **protein** daily — more protein depending on your weight. Establishing good eating habits now can help prevent illnesses such as *osteoporosis* (bone disease) and heart disease later in life. Good foods are also needed to keep your body strong as it goes through the dramatic growth spurts of puberty.

Adolescent girls have special, additional nutritional needs. A big area of concern is **iron**. While girls are menstruating, they lose almost *twice* as much iron a month as boys. Drinking colas or beverages that contain caffeine, or eating chocolate, can make things worse by slowing down iron absorption.

Calcium is another mineral girls especially need. That's because calcium is lost in the monthly menstrual flow.

Although there is not yet any minimum daily requirement set for **potassium**, it is a mineral that you should make sure you get every day. Some experts recommend 2,000 mg. Eat bananas, oranges, white meat chicken. Without enough potassium, you can feel weak, light-headed and irritable, especially around your period.

Can You Have Too Many Vitamins And Minerals?

Although as an adolescent female you have special needs for certain vitamins and minerals, you must be careful about how you get them, and how many you take. Some girls are so concerned that they won't get enough that they take vitamin pills by the fistful. These girls can make themselves seriously ill, because overdosing on some vitamins can have toxic effects.

Other girls use vitamins as substitutes for eating. To them, a vitamin pill and a cup of tea is a perfectly adequate meal. These girls are making a foolish mistake.

Let's start with the basics. Most doctors agree that taking a multiple vitamin and mineral pill to supplement a good, nutritious daily diet is probably not a bad idea. Vitamins should be used a supplements, not as substitutes. Why? Your body also needs other elements present in foods— for instance fiber, or so-called "trace" elements such as zinc.

Taking a megadose of a single vitamin or mineral can have negative consequences on your body. For instance, too much calcium can harm your body's ability to absorb iron. Low iron is enough of a problem for women already.

Over a period of time, taking too much Vitamin C can decrease you body's ability to absorb copper. That can lead to anemia. Too much Vitamin A can cause serious problems including headaches, hair loss, scaly skin and liver damage.

> **TIP:** Eat a wide variety of foods. It's the best way of ensuring a good balance of vitamins and minerals.

Vitamin and Mineral Needs for Teenage Girls

Vitamin/Mineral	Daily Need	Source	Why Needed
Calcium	1,000-1,200 mg	Dairy products	Bone formation Healthy teeth
Iron	18 grams	Liver, red meat, raisins	Red blood cell production
Vitamin A	5,000 International Units	Green/yellow vegetables: carrots, tomatoes, cheese	Good vision Bone/teeth formation
Vitamin D	400 IU	Fish, sunlight, egg yolks, fortified milk	Healthy heart Healthy nervous system
Vitamin E	12-15 IU's	Milk, eggs, fish, meats, cereals, nuts, vegetables	Red blood cell production
Vitamin K	5-100 mg	Spinach, bran, rice, tomatoes	Blood coagulation
Vitamin B1 (Thiamine)	Approx. 1 mg	Pork, beef, liver, whole or enriched grains, beans	Healthy nervous system
Vitamin B2 (Riboflavin)	1-1.5 mg	Milk, liver, enriched cereals, cheese	Red blood cell formation
Vitamin B3 (Niacin)	14-20 mg	Meat, peanuts, enriched grains	Healthy nervous system, brain function
Vitamin B6 (Pyroxine)	2 mg	Corn, wheat germ, lean meats, bananas	Helps reduce cramps Promotes healthy skin
Folic Acid	400 mg	Green leafy vegetables, asparagus, liver, kidneys	Formation of red blood cells
Vitamin B12	3 mg	Lean meat, milk, eggs, cheese, liver	Promotes growth Improves concentration
Vitamin C	45 mg	Citrus fruits, tomatoes, cabbage, potatoes, broccoli, strawberries	Heals wounds Strengthens blood vessels Helps ward off infection

SANITARY PROTECTION AND HYGIENE

When you look in the sanitary supplies section of the drugstore, you may be overwhelmed by shelves and shelves of boxes. How do you know which brand to choose? How do you know what kind of protection is best in the first place?

First of all, let's look at your choices. There are two main types of protection: pads and tampons.

Pads These are used externally. They come in a variety of shapes and thicknesses. Most have adhesive strips to keep them in place inside your underwear. Every brand can do the job, but there are a few differences. Some have tiny dimples for "extra absorbency." Some have side panels to prevent leaking. Experiment until you find a brand you like. Don't use "pantyliner" types except on very light days.

Tampons These are used internally. They are made of absorbent material. The tampon is then compressed in a plastic or cardboard tube, which is used to insert the tampon into the vagina. Because the use of tampons in the super size has been linked to a disorder called Toxic Shock Syndrome, most medical experts recommend the use of regular or light size tampons.

TIP: Avoid deodorized pads or tampons. They are no more effective and they can cause irritation.

YOUR CHANGING FEELINGS

With all those dramatic changes going on inside and outside your body, it's no surprise that your feelings take you on a wild roller-coaster ride too. Intense, quickly changing emotions and moods are as much a part of puberty as breast development.

Why? Remember, your body is building a new chemical system. It affects everything about you, including feelings.

For another thing, you're developing a mature personality. A grown-up you is being born to replace the little kid you once were. The process isn't simple because *you* aren't simple. Human personalities are complicated. To fully develop your personality, you might go through some mixed-up reactions — liking someone one minute, disliking her the next; being happy, and then suddenly sad. It's the only way you can finally sort out exactly how you *do* feel about things and figure out who you really are.

Learning to Like Yourself

Many teens are their own worst enemies. They can't find anything good to say about themselves. Instead, they focus on all the mistakes they make and all the "dumb" things they do.

Everyone makes mistakes. It's the only way to learn. This long transition period between childhood and adulthood is designed for experimenting and exploring. Mistakes are just part of the process.

It's important to learn to like yourself in your teens. Don't be conceited, just to keep in mind all the positive, good things about *you*. A good self image is crucial to success and happiness all through your life. Read through the following questions. They'll help single out some good things about yourself. Write your responses on a piece of paper. (There are no right or wrong answers, of course.)

1. Two things that made me happy this week were...

2. Two ways I made people happy this week were...

3. My favorite things to do with my family and friends are...

4. A particular skill or talent I have is...

5. Two reasons why people would like being my friend are...

Feelings About Parents

Are you feeling a little different about your parents lately? A little...negative?

At your age, it's not unusual to start finding fault with your folks. Little habits they have, like the old-fashioned way they dress or the music they like, may really begin to bug you. Maybe they seem to be tightening up on you. They won't leave you alone. They want to know every move you make.

It's easy to be super-critical of parents when you're an adolescent. Because *you're* trying to become independent at the same time they're trying to establish rules and guidelines to protect and help you, some real explosions can occur.

You can do something about it. You can make these tough times a little easier by doing something very simple: *talking*.

Let your parents know how you're feeling and what you're doing. Share some of the highlights of your day. You don't have to tell them *every* little thing, but at least give them the flavor of what school was like, what people are talking about, etc. And ask them about *their* days.

If you're unhappy about something at home — for instance, you don't have enough privacy — talk it out. Maybe you can figure something out together, like building a colorful screen to give you your own section of a shared bedroom. Maybe everyone can arrange to let you have privacy at certain times.

Your parents love you a lot, but they aren't mind-readers. They're only human. So start talking.

> **TIP:** Remember, hostility meets with hostility. Talk to your parents in a quiet voice. More can be accomplished through quiet reasoning than angry shouting.

Feelings About Boys

For years, you've played with them and gone to school with them and they were no big deal. Now you feel attracted to boys. You want to be around them. They're interesting, even though they can make you feel shy and tongue-tied.

If it's any comfort, boys are feeling just as funny around you. When an attraction to the opposite sex is felt for the first time, no one is quite sure how to handle it. It can cause a lot of worry.

Girls worry about whether boys will ever like them. Boys worry too. In fact, they may worry more. It's just that in our culture, boys don't tend to talk about things like this as much as girls.

Crushes are common during puberty. Just be prepared: the object of your affection may not return those feelings. He may think you're a nice kid, or a good student, and that's all. The teenage years are a wonderful time for meeting different people and developing a wide variety of friendships. Tying yourself down to one person can stifle all that.

If you like boys and want to have a boyfriend, concentrate on being a *friend* to boys. Be a good listener and a good sport. Keep yourself involved in activities. Don't turn into a boring person who only thinks about "getting" a boy. Boys like to be with people who are fun and enthusiastic about life. You go about having a boyfriend the same way you go about having a girlfriend — by being someone people want to spend time with. It's that simple.

BIBLIOGRAPHY

What's Happening to My Body?, Lynda Madaras with Area Madaras. New-Market Press, New York.

The New Teenage Body Book, Kathy McCoy and Charles Wibbelsman, M.D. The Body Press, Los Angeles.

PMS and You, Niels H. Lauersen, M.D., and Eileen Stukane. Fireside Books (A division of Simon and Schuster), New York.

Vitamin Bible for Your Kids, Earl Mindell. Bantam Books, New York.

The Woman Doctor's Diet for Teen-Age Girls, Barbara Edelstein, M.D. Ballantine Books, New York.

The American Medical Association Family Medical Guide, Editor-in-Chief, Jeffrey R.M. Kunz, M.D. Random House, New York.

"Girl to Woman: A Growing-Up Guide," A. Bell. Teen, November 1987 (and issues following), p. 50.

"Test Your Breasts," J.C. Johnson, Mademoiselle. November 1987, p. 150.

"Cramps," Kathy McCoy, Seventeen. June 1987, p. 38.

"How Exercise Can K-O Your Period," S. Festa, Mademoiselle. August 1987, p. 120.

"Menstruation: That Time of the Month," Teen. March 1987, p. 80.

"All About Breasts," Kathy McCoy, Seventeen. October 1987, p. 46.

"Body Basics," Issues of Teen Magazine beginning November 1987.

"Body Talk," Seventeen. August 1986, p. 254.

INDEX